My Visit To The SEASIDE

Diana Bentley

Reading Consultant
University of Reading

Photographs by
Paul Seheult

Wayland

My Visit

First Published in 1989 by
Wayland (Publishers) Limited
61 Western Road, Hove
East Sussex, BN3 1JD, England

© Copyright 1989 Wayland (Publishers) Limited

Editor: Sophie Davies

British Library Cataloguing in Publication Data

Bentley, Diana
  My visit to the seaside.
  1. English language reader. - For children
  I. Title II. Seheult, Paul
  428.6

ISBN 1 85210 713 8

Typeset by: Lizzie George, Wayland
Printed and bound by Casterman S.A., Belgium

Contents

All words that appear in **bold** are explained in the glossary on page 22.

Hello, my name is Ben.

Today it is hot and sunny, and we are going to the seaside. I take all the toys from the sandpit. I put them in a bag for the beach. Mum and Dad help us to put everything in the car. Now we are ready to go.

Here comes the little train.

At the seaside there is a little railway. Nick and I wait for the train. Here it comes! There is a steering wheel in our carriage, so I pretend to be the train driver.

Now we go to the beach.

We get off the train and go to the beach. We take off our shirts and shoes, and put on swimming trunks. Dad and Nick collect pebbles. Nick puts them in his bucket. He stands on the **breakwater**, and pours the pebbles back in the sea.

I play in the sea with my friends.

These are my new friends. I met them on the beach. We go in the sea together. The water is almost up to my waist. My friend climbs on the breakwater. We like it when the big waves splash us.

I find a crab and a **starfish**.

We walk along the beach. There are some **rockpools**. I catch a crab with my fishing net. I hold it in my hand. It does not look very happy, so I put it back in the water. Then I find a starfish. Look at its five pointed legs!

We walk along the **pier**.

We leave the beach and walk along the pier. There are lots of things to see and do. We find a funny picture. We put our heads through the holes. The picture makes Mum and Dad look like children.

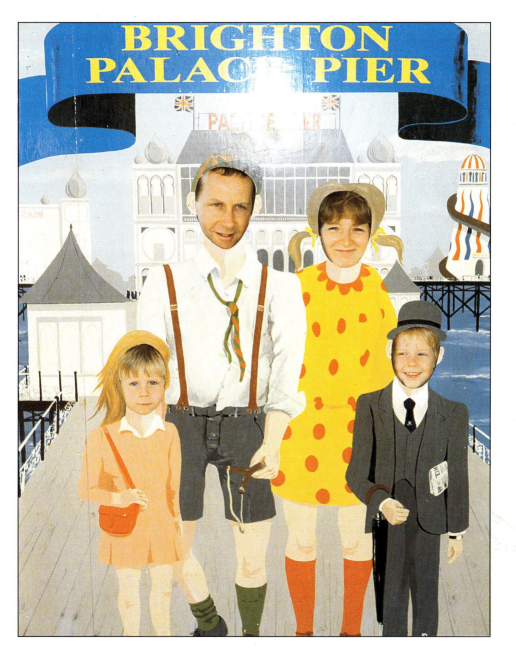

15

We have hot dogs for lunch.

Now we are very hungry. We find a hot dog stall on the pier. Mum and Dad buy some. We sit down and eat our lunch. Nick gets tomato sauce all over his face!

We go on the helter skelter.

Dad takes me on the helter skelter. Dad pays and the man gives us a mat each. We climb up the stairs and sit on our mats at the top of the slide. The slide goes round and round and we go faster and faster. Here we come!

Now it is time to go home.

It is time to go home but first we buy an ice cream. We leave the pier and walk back to the car. Mum drives us home. Here we are, back in our garden. Nick is very tired. We have had a lovely day at the seaside.

Glossary

Breakwater   A strong wall that goes out to sea. It stops the sea from wearing away the land.

Pier   A long platform that goes out to sea. It has games and rides, and shops selling sweets and food.

Rockpool   A pool of water in the rocks on the beach. It often has strange plants and animals in it.

Starfish   A type of fish you find on the beach. It is shaped like a star, with five pointed legs.

Books to read

Katy Goes to the Seaside (Macdonald, 1988)
My Class Goes to the Seaside Jill Flanders
  and Charles Harris (Franklin Watts, 1986)
On the Seashore Sarah McKenzie (Wayland,
  1985)

Acknowledgements

The author and publishers would like to thank
Rosie and Bruce, Ben and Nick Murray for
their help with this book.

Index